A

STUDY

OF

FREEMASONRY.

TRANSLATED FROM THE FRENCH

OF

MONSEIGNEUR DUPANLOUP,

BISHOP OF ORLEANS.

PREFACE OF TRANSLATOR.

IN presenting the following translation of Mgr Dupanloup's pamphlet on Freemasonry to the English public, at the personal request of the Venerable Prelate himself, two objections will have to be met : the first, that the fearful revelations contained in it do not affect English Freemasonry, which is supposed to be totally distinct and different from the Society called by the same name abroad ; the second, that the warning is addressed to Catholics only, whose dogmas and principles are in distinct contradiction to the lines of modern thought, and directly opposed to so-called modern progress ; so that the warning does not apply to the English nation, who, as a body, are Protestants. Both these objections have been so ably treated in a book recently published, entitled the *Secret Warfare of Freemasonry against Church and State*, translated from the German, that we should hesitate to do more than refer our readers to this most admirable and exhaustive work, were it not for the fact that many may take up this pamphlet who will have neither the time to read nor the means to purchase the volume in question ; so that we shall venture to make certain quotations from its pages in meeting the two grave objections to which we have referred.

The first question to ask ourselves is this : Is there, or

is there not, a solidarity between English and foreign Lodges ?

Now no satisfactory answer to this can be given except by referring to the Freemasons themselves ; and our reply will, therefore, be based on their own statements.

The ritual for the admission of a Scotch Ancient, or Grand Master, runs as follows :

'Friendship is the sacred bond which unites together all the Brethren of our Craft ; for however much scattered they may be over the face of the earth, they all compose one only body, because one is their origin and one their aim ; one the mysteries into which they are initiated ; one the path by which they are led ; one the gauge and measure applied to each and all of them ; and one the spirit by which they are animated.'*

The same unity of aim and object is, we think, incontestably proved by the public proceedings which took place at the installation of H.R.H. the Prince of Wales as Grand Master of English Freemasons. On that occasion he received addresses of congratulation from the 'Grand Orient Lodge' of France, from the 'Grand Lodge' of Italy, from that of Sweden, and many other countries. We will only quote one of these addresses, which will suffice for our purpose—that of the 'Grand Italian' Lodge. It is headed as follows :

'*Universal Freemasonry. Italian Communion, Liberty, Fraternity, Equality. . . .*

'May it please your Royal Highness to permit the Grand Master of the Grand Orient of Italy to unite the

---

* Eckert, *Die Trage der Staatl. Anerk.* p. 12 (Barrister in Dresden. Leipzig, 1852).

heartfelt applause of all our Italian brethren to that of our beloved brethren in England, who hail the elevation of their puissant Grand Master as one of the most auspicious and most memorable events of universal Masonry.

'By this event English Masonry, which has already deserved so well of universal humanity, will acquire ever fresh titles to the gratitude and admiration of the whole civilized world. Italian Masonry, therefore, rejoices at this new lustre shed upon *our world-wide Institution*, and sincerely prays that between the two Masonic communities may be drawn *ever more closely* those fraternal ties which, through want of that *official* recognition which we venture to hope will soon be effected, have always bound us to our English brethren, whose profound intelligence and unwearying activity we constantly appreciate and seek to follow.

'Accept then, Royal Highness, with all great wishes for your continued long life and prosperity, the expression of our profound homage and fraternal affection. . . .'

The '*official* recognition' prayed for in this address was not long delayed. In an account of the consecration of a new Lodge in July last we find the following announcement in the *Times* (of 19th July 1875):

'ITALIAN AND ENGLISH FREEMASONS.—The announcement was made on Saturday, at the consecration of a new lodge, named after the Princess of Wales, at the Alexandra Palace, that his Royal Highness the Grand Master of English Freemasons had given official recognition to the Grand Orient of Italy, and the announcement was received with warm applause by the large body of eminent Freemasons assembled on the occasion.'

We do not think, therefore, that the fact can be denied,

that the 'Brotherhood' is substantially one in all lands.

Another significant fact, which adds to the weight of proof already given, is the appointment by 'the Most Worshipful Grand Master,' after his installation, of Brother Wendt to be Grand Secretary for GERMAN CORRESPONDENCE. Were there no solidarity between the Lodges, of what use would be the secretary?

But the main objection which has been made to the identification of English Freemasonry with the political and religious tenets of foreign Lodges is derived from the roll of names, partly illustrious by position and partly distinguished by high public and private worth, which is to be found in the archives of the Society.

'How is it possible,' writes the author we have already mentioned,* 'that emperors, kings, and princes (and we would add English gentlemen of noble birth and unblemished character) would persevere in lending the sanction of their name to a body one of whose acknowledged objects is to overthrow every throne in Europe, and extirpate all social distinctions throughout the world?'

We will give the answer in the same author's words: 'The reply is obvious: *they have been deceived, and continue in the dark.* It is thoroughly understood among the secret heads and chief agents of the body that such brethren would not remain a single day in union with such a league if they were aware of its ultimate designs; so they have established for their convenience special degrees of honor and offices of seeming authority, where

---

* *Secret Warfare of Freemasonry,* Introduction, 1.

they may attract the uninitiated by the authority of their high character and exalted position, without enfeebling the secret action of "the Craft" by the demurrers of an over-scrupulous morality. The great universities of this realm are wont to confer on distinguished generals, authors, and other celebrities the honorary degree of doctor of civil law; but it is not commonly supposed that those who are selected for such a distinction have any deep knowledge of this particular branch of jurisprudence.' *

* If any one wishes to be still further convinced of the solidarity of Freemasonry all over the world, let him read an article in the *Daily Telegraph* on this subject, in a leader of 2 th April 18.5. Another contemporary newspaper, speaking of Freemasonry, writes as follows : 'Hard as it is for men to believe that it is so diabolical abroad, it is harder still, it is simply impossible, for them to think it other than a mere "friendly society' at home, when thousands well known for their principles, for hon r and honesty of purpose in their own circles, have willingly, nay gladly, placed their names on the rolls of its various English Lodges. Englishmen, loyal and Protestant, could never lend themselves or their names to support the ends for which Freemasonry is said to exist; yet many such are actually Masons, and sworn members of that same Society which is so numerous and so widespread abroad. That ociety, then, cannot be the evil it is said to be ; or else Freemasonry here is not the same as elsewhere. This latter woul 1 appear to be the general opinion, and to rest upon a basis of something like fact ; for the Craft is too wary to overlook the English love for law and order, too sharp not to recognize in this character an obstacle to its own final success, and too cautious theref re, to admit any but those who have been well tried and sounded to a knowledge of its present actions and future aims. Here, as abroad, the multitude of the brotherhood have little more idea of the scope of Freemasonry than the general public has ; they are kept at play in the antechamber, like children in the nursery, whilst real business is transacted in the

But a still stronger testimony is that of one of the most eminent of the French Freemasons, M. Louis Blanc, whose words have been quoted by Mgr. Dupanloup in the following pamphlet, but which we shall make no apology for repeating here. He says :

'It seemed good to sovereigns—to Frederick the Great —to handle the trowel and to put on the apron. Why not ? Since the existence of the higher grades was carefully hidden from them, *all they knew of Freemasonry was that which could be revealed to them without danger.* They had no reason for concerning themselves about it, seeing that they were kept in the lower grades' (though *nominally* the highest), 'in which they perceived nothing but an opportunity for amusement, joyful banquets, principles forsaken and resumed at the threshold of the Lodges, formulas that had no reference to ordinary life —in a word, a comedy of equality. But in these matters comedy closely borders on tragedy ; and princes and nobles were induced to *offer the cover of their names and the blind aid of their influence* to secret undertakings directed against themselves.'*

'Can any reasonable man doubt, after reading such an explicit admission as this, that kings and princes, statesmen and legislators, may be found in grades of high

i ner chambers by the o'der members of the family. Men are slow to allow that they can be duped, and it will be no easy matter to get those who have joined the Craft to relinquish their membership, or to deter those from joining it who are so inclined, on the strength of what certainly is, to say the least of it, a well-founded suspicio of dark dealings But the question is not a matter of mere judgment or prudence ; it is one of morality and co science.'

* *Study of Freemasonry,* page 65. French edition.

honor and dignity—provided by Freemasonry for their
especial benefit—may assume the first place in its public
manifestations and the *external* direction of its government, and may yet remain in ignorance of its hidden
designs as unconscious and complete as that of the "*profane*," who are altogether excluded from its Lodges ?'
(Introduction *Secret Warfare*.)

In spite of all their caution, however, the real nature
of Freemason doctrines occasionally becomes revealed
to their noble dupes ; and an instance of this is to be
found in the resignation of Frederick Prince of Orange,
second son of William I., King of the Netherlands, who
had been chosen on the 4th June 1816 (when he had
scarcely attained his nineteenth year) as National Grand
Master for life of the Grand Lodge of the Hague. The
next year he was elected, in the Grand Orient in Brussels, to the Grand Mastership of the Southern—now
called the Belgian—Lodges. Although he had only been
made acquainted with a very small portion of the impious legendary teaching of the Craft, yet that little was
enough. He resigned his dignities instantly, and alleged
the following reasons, of which we will give a short extract : 'I am a Christian, and will ever remain one.
Everybody will understand how extremely painful it is
for me to be compelled to speak of the abuse made in
the Masonic Legend of the teaching of my Divine Master, the Son of the Heavenly Father. . . How could
I write the story of Thy life, O Divine Jesus, and then
call it the *Legend of the Degree of Rosicrucian?* . . .
Right reason and profound reverence bid my pen stop
here. Is it possible to degrade this hallowed story so
low as to turn it into a mere legend ? . . . And can

it be that the brethren of the Craft regard the death of Jesus Christ as a mere parable, and range it with the mass of fictions which are successively set before them ? . . . And we further find, to our indignation, cere-monies in connection with the reading of the legend of this grade which are in direct opposition to the teach-ing and character of the Son of God and to His Holy Law. . . .'

How many of those excellent religious-minded men who have given 'the cover of their names,' as Louis Blanc calls it, to this impious and dangerous society would recoil with horror, like Prince Frederick, could they but once lift the veil which shrouds the real aim and object of Freemasonry ?

But there is a further point to be considered.

'To promise silence with regard to teaching and a course of action about which we know absolutely no-thing at the time we make the promise, is intrinsically evil. When, moreover, this secrecy is enforced by the sanction of an oath—the most solemn and indissoluble bond by which the freedom of the human will can be fettered—the heinousness of the crime is proportion-ably increased.' Read the Masonic oath as given, not only in the following pamphlet, but in every Freemason ritual. 'Is it not in violation of the natural order, and an ever-present menace to political stability, that a body of men should exist within the State bound by obedience to an unknown and irresponsible authority, and shielded from all possible supervision either of constituted au-thority or public opinion, by so awful an oath of secrecy? "I consider," says Lord Plunket, "an association bound by a secret oath to be extremely dangerous on the principles of the common law, inasmuch as they subtract the subject from the State, and interpose between him and his allegiance to the king." And he speaks most truly, for it is an act of high treason against the most fundamental principles of political and social life, which forbid us to abdicate the freedom of our will in favor of an unknown and self-constituted authority, or to bind ourselves irrevocably to the propagation of tenets or to the blind execution of orders about which we are in utter ignorance at the time, and are therefore unable to determine whether they be consistent or not with our moral obligations to ourselves, our neighbors, and our God.' *

But now to come to the second objection—namely, that the Bishop's pamphlet, being intended merely for Catholics, the warnings it contains do not apply to the English nation, who, as a body, are Protestants.

Again we will answer this objection from the mouths of the Freemasons themselves.

We are prepared to prove that Freemasonry is not the enemy of Catholicity alone, but of Christianity in general : and a bitter and irreconcilable enemy to every species of Divine Revelation. The following important admission is found in what may be called an official apology for the Association :

'Freemasonry teaches how to be virtuous without the stimulus of hope or fear, independently alike of heaven or hell. The Mason looks for no future reward : he has received his recompense in the present, and is therewith content.' †

---

* *Secret Warfare of Freemasonry*, Introduction, lvii. lviii.
† *The Attitude of Freemasonry in Relation to the Present Day ; or*

Preface of Translator.

Again : respecting the Bible in the Lodges, an article appears in the official Dutch Freemason's Almanac for 1872, by Brother C. Von Schaick, from which we take the following extracts :

'As matters now stand, the presence of the Bible on our altars is an empty form. . . . From whatever point of view we regard the Bible, we do not hesitate to declare openly that in our reunions it is out of place, once and for ever ; since the doctrines of humanity now occupy the most prominent position, and are taught as the best method of ameliorating the condition of mankind.'

Another Brother, C. Krause, speaks thus : 'However Masons may formerly have regarded the Bible, they now, at all events, know how to put it in its proper place. The Mason should be entirely free from all blind adhesion to any dogmatic belief whatsoever, just as Jesus appears to have been,' etc., etc.   These are only one or two quotations out of many in the same sense, and we ask what are called Bible Christians if they can take one step in union with an Association which altogether repudiates the divine origin of Holy Writ, and sees in it nothing but an accessory to a ceremonial ?

But the attitude of Freemasonry in regard to the Divinity of Christ is even more serious.   The 'Secret International Congress of Freemasons,' held during the first three days of November 1872, determined to give, if possible, the force of constitutional law to the opinions of Freemasonry as to what ought to be called religion.

an Open Exposure of the Object and History of Freemasonry, together with an Answer to the most recent Charges brought against it. By E. E. Eckert, Barrister in Dresden. Leipzig, 1852.

' The congress met at a villa near Lugano, and sat each day from 4 P.M. until midnight. One of the subjects deliberated upon was the nature of the worship to be introduced. It was unanimously agreed to throw into a catechetical shape the democratic Bible of the Socinian Renan, and to make this the handbook of the religion to be publicly recognized in the social and democratic Republic of the future.' * Again : the *Freemason's Journal of Vienna* (2d series, No. 2, p. 143) thus reports the speech of a Master addressing his brethren from the chair of office :

' What is the false religion so eagerly forced upon mankind in mosques, synagogues, temples, and churches, except a jugglery carried on by Imaums, Popes, and clergy ? Are we to hold our tongues about it all, till defective education, long habits of slavery, superstitious prejudices, and unreasoning endurance shall at length have deprived men even of the power to see the real state of affairs ? '

But this is not all.

Le Globe, a Masonic journal issued from 1839 to 1843 by L. T. Juge (one who had himself been initiated into the highest grades of Freemasonry), has been pronounced by those invested with the highest authority in the Craft to be the truest exponent of its secret teaching. In this journal an account is given of a speech delivered in the Lodge of the Knights of Malta by ' Brother' de Branville (officer of the Grand Orient of France) on the religion of the Craft, of which we will only extract the first sentence :

---

* *Secret Warfare,* pp. 6–8.

Preface of Translator.

1. 'The religious tenets of Freemasonry are only a continuation of the Egyptian doctrines transmitted to successive generations by the priests of the Temple of Isis.'

Then follows a long explanation of the history and derivation of these Pagan mysteries; Brother Nash going on to explain (in an article which appeared in the *English Freemason's Quarterly Review*) how Freemasonry derives its origin from the mysteries of Isis and Osiris. Commenting upon this, the *Globe*, after descanting on 'the last effort they are making to rally their forces for a supreme struggle with Christianity,' continues : ' An association speedily formed itself, which, in opposition to the universal faith of Europe at that time, took upon itself to recognize the existence only of a God whose being is coeval with that of matter, who is incapable of division into a plurality of persons, who is not subject to human infirmities, and consequently neither has died nor can die. . . . And would not our supposition ' (as to the origin of the Craft) ' be yet more triumphantly proved, if to this elementary doctrine another were added, namely, that Christ could not have been God, but was merely a being of superior intelligence, a philosopher, a sage, a benefactor of humanity ? and if it were asserted that miracles must necessarily be rejected as a violation of the eternal and immutable laws of the universe, alike impossible and needless, God requiring no such means of enforcing the obedience of His creatures ? *And are not these doctrines*, which indisputably derive their origin immediately from Gnosticism, *the fundamental principles of Freemasonry?* Does the Freemason divide into several persons the Incomprehensible Being whom he denominates the "Supreme Architect" of all worlds ? Does he believe that death was or ever could be possible to this Supreme Being ? . . .'

' Thus we find the Most Holy Trinity, the Divinity of Christ, together with all that follows from that doctrine, the possibility of miracles—in a word, the whole scheme of Christianity—denied by the organ of Freemasonry in its name and with its approval.'* Is it then to be wondered at that the Protestant Consistory of Hanover in 1745 declared that any preacher who was already a Freemason should be compelled immediately to resign his membership and abandon all practices connected with it ? and that, in future, all clergy should be forbidden, under strict penalties, to join the Craft ? And the same was enacted by the Lutheran Congress at Kammin.

We could multiply instances of the horrible impiety and coarse rationalism propounded in the Lodges, where ' The Saviour adored by Christians is represented as being a common Jew of Bethlehem, who was confounded with the ancient Josue, son of Nun, by the credulous and barbarous Druses of the Lebanon, and afterwards exalted to be the God of Christendom by the Western Popes for the furtherance of their own selfish aims.'†

But lest this Preface should stretch to an unwarrantable length, we will only give one or two more extracts from Freemason authorities : the first from a publication originally written in High German, of which a Dutch translation appeared in 1792—a work all the more

---

* *Secret Warfire*, p. 74.   † Ibid. p. 199.

worthy of credence, as it is supported by documentary evidence. *

'1. Superstition (*i.e.*, Christianity and the Law of Moses) has hitherto been the mainstay of the tyranny and deception by means of which princes and priests have drawn mankind into their net. Fear of a future life, of an eternity of punishments, had been a motive powerful enough to hold weak minds, bowed down under the load of prejudices sucked in with their mother's milk, and to enervate the boldest spirits, rendering them incapable of any great action. This is the evil of Christianity, that it enslaves minds to such a point that they are willing to endure any present suffering with the consoling hope of a life to come. On this account it becomes indispensable to undermine the pillar which bears up such a structure of superstition. But as the number of those who yet fondly cling to the pious fictions of their childhood is very large, and the roots of political and civil institutions strike deep in the national soil, it is necessary to go cautiously to work. Here philosophy may take a useful hint from nature. As man is chiefly worked on through his passions, these must be excited, and Christianity must be made ridiculous ere the dominion of faith can be overthrown in the heart.

'2. To effect this a literary association must be formed,

---

* Reprinted at the Hague in 1823 (*Secret Warfare*). According to the opinion expressed by the Dutch translator, the author of this work, which at the time created a great sensation was a Professor Hoffmann of Vienna, editor of the *Wiener Zeitschrift.* The German title is given in full in *Secret Warfare,* p 82.

to promote the circulation of our writings, and suppress as far as possible those of our opponents.

'3. For this end we must contrive to have in our pay the publishers of the leading literary journals of the day, in order that they may turn into ridicule and heap contempt on everything written in a contrary interest to our own.

'4. "He that is not with us is against us." Therefore we may persecute, calumniate, and tread down such a one without scruple : individuals like this are noxious insects, which one shakes from the blossoming tree and crushes beneath one's foot.

'5. Very few can bear to be made to look ridiculous ; let ridicule, therefore, be the weapon employed against persons who, though by no means devoid of sense, show themselves hostile to our schemes.

'6. In order the more quickly to attain our end, the middle classes of society must be thoroughly imbued with our principles ; the lower orders and the mass of the population are of little importance, as they may easily be moulded to our will. The middle classes are the principal supporters of the Government ; to gain them we must work on their passions, and above all bring up the rising generation in our ideas, as in a few years they will be, in their turn, masters of the situation.

'7. License in morals will be the best means of enabling us to provide ourselves with patrons at court, persons who are nevertheless totally ignorant of the importance of our cause. It will suffice for our purpose if we make them absolutely indifferent to the Christian religion. They are, for the most part, careless enough without us.

'8. If our aims are to be pursued with vigor, it is of absolute necessity to regard as enemies of enlightenment and of philosophy all those who cling in any way to religious or civil prejudice, and exhibit this attachment in their writings. They must be viewed as beings whose influence is highly prejudicial to the human race, and a great obstacle to its well-being and progress. On this account it becomes the duty of each one of us to impede their action in all matters of consequence, and to seize the first suitable opportunity which may present itself of putting them entirely *hors de combat.*

'9. We must ever be on the watch to make all changes in the State serve our own ends; political parties, cabals, brotherhoods, unions—in short, everything that affords an opportunity of creating disturbances must be an instrument in our hands. For it is only on the ruins of society, as it exists at present, that we can hope to erect a solid structure on the natural system, and ensure to the worshippers of nature the free exercise of their rights.'

We leave these revelations to the consideration of our English readers. Of one thing there is no doubt—that the key-note of Freemasonry is war to the death against all revelation. As far back as the end of the preceding century it expressed itself in these terms :

'Belief in revelation is a malady to which weak and pious minds are very subject; it is an infectious epidemic, employed ever since the world began to effect the destruction of human liberty; it is alike incompatible with sound reason and true freedom; it is the parent of fanaticism and superstition.' 'The laws of the Mosaic and Christian religions are the contemptible inventions of petty minds bent on deceiving others ; they are the most extravagant aberrations of the human intellect.' 'The selfishness of the clergy and the despotism of the great have for centuries upheld this system (of Christianity), since it enabled them to rule mankind with a rod of iron by means of its rigid code of morality ; and to confirm their power over weak minds by certain oracular utterances, in reality the product of their own invention, but palmed off on the world as the words of revelation.'*

'The grade of Kadosch,' writes Barruel, 'is the soul of Freemasonry ; and the final object of its plots is the reintroduction of absolute liberty and equality through the destruction of all royalty and *the abrogation of all religious worship.'* †

We now leave English Protestants to decide for themselves whether the designs of Freemasonry are directed against the Church of Rome *alone.*

NOTE.—It has been objected to Mgr. Dupanloup's pamphlet in some quarters that many of his quotations are taken from newspapers, such as the *Monde-Maçonnique,* the *Globe,* the *Freemason's Journal,* the *Chain of Union,* and the like. But if these Freemason organs do not represent aright the doctrines and proceedings of the Craft, why do they continue to exist ? Every distinct form of political or religious belief has its organ in the public press ; and if any one of these were an unfair or untruthful exponent of its principles or its actions, its

---

* *Waarschuwing,* vol. xi., Nos. 1, 2, 8, quoted by the *Secret Warfare* on p. 207.

† Barruel's *Mémoires du Jacobinisme,* vol ii. p. 282. His testimony is valuable, as he was a Master Mason.

circulation would consequently fall off, and the paper itself die a natural death. We beg to call our English readers' attention to the *Chain of Union*, and other quotations from English Freemason periodicals, which prove that they are not a whit behind their brethren on the Continent in their 'advanced' views of so-called progress.

We would call attention also to a striking and forcible article on ' *Freemasonry*,' in the ' *Month and Catholic Review*' *for September* 1875. It appeared only after the present work was in type, and we were therefore unable either to refer to it in the body of our preface, or to quote, as we should otherwise have done, certain salient passages. It has been received from a source which may be regarded as a guarantee for its authenticity ; and bears the signature 'Joabert M. M.' Though written from an Anglican, rather than a Catholic, point of view, it has been refused insertion in more than one Protestant organ of influence, on account, we may fairly presume, of its candid witness about the tendency of Freemasonry. While directing special notice to the article as a whole, we content ourselves with the following brief quotation as connected with our own universities : 'At Oxford and Cambridge, the University lodges (for such is the fraternal feeling that the University Lodge will not have any fellowship with the Town Lodge) would be comparatively empty, but for recruits among the undergraduates ; and so " dispensations " are granted by the Grand Lodge to enable young men *under age* to become Freemasons.'

CONTENTS.

Contents.

THIRD PART.

POLITICAL AND REVOLUTIONARY ACTION OF FREE-MASONRY.

CONCLUSION.

A

STUDY OF FREEMASONRY.

EVERY one knows Freemasonry by name. I knew of
it like all the rest of the world ; but for a long time I have
wished to study it more closely, and several motives
urged me in the same direction, especially M. de Persigny's famous circular. It is an undeniable fact that,
since that circular appeared, Freemasonry has entered
upon a new phase in France. Until then, shrouded in
mystery, it only worked in the dark ; but, thanks to the
encouragement given to it by the Imperial Government,
it has since that time come forward, as it were, into
public life ; and its proselytism, always ardent, but formerly cautious and circumspect, is become more fer-
vent still : it has published books, started periodicals
founded a number of new lodges, made a far larger
number of recruits, lifted its banner on high ; and only
the other day, a Freemason at one of the lodges dwelt

emphatically on 'the rapid invasion of the whole world by Freemason doctrines.' *

It would, in fact, be superfluous to deny the progress of the movement ; or to dissimulate its daily increasing influence, and the hidden but real part it has taken in contemporary revolutions.

When one sees the preponderating *rôle* which Freemasonry plays the morning after those serious catastrophes which, in a moment, make a radical change in the political and social condition of a whole people ; when one considers the part it takes in those sudden triumphs of violence in which it is ever ready to furnish both chiefs and soldiers, it is difficult to believe that it has nothing to say to them : and the study which I have made of the subject has proved to me, by the strongest possible evidence, that the strangest solidarity and the gravest responsibilities rest upon it.

* The *Monde-Maçonnique*, May 1870. p. 118. According to a statement (probably exaggerated) made by the same organ, 'There exist at this moment n France 400,000 Freemasons. In this number women are not included' *Ibid.* p. 212. The *Monde-Maçonnique*, which publishes this document, does not attempt to deny it ; and we read in the *Constitution Maçonnique Française*, ART. 5, that ' *Freemasonry hopes eventually to embrace every member of humanity.*'

It is, then, impossible that such an institution should find us indifferent to its existence, or that we should hesitate to speak frankly of what we believe to be the truth.

The hour is arrived when it has become a duty for us, after having thoroughly enquired into the subject ourselves, to enlighten those who ought to know the real state of the case.

For Freemasonry has its deceptions, by means of which it deludes its votaries, and which explain to a certain degree the singular attraction it has for the good men whom it deceives. For there are two kinds of adepts in this society those who do not know its ultimate aim or object ; and those, the real Freemasons, who know perfectly well what they are about, and, what it is that they are doing and aiming at.

I have often been asked the following questions on the subject of Freemasonry :

Is it an institution hostile to religion ?

May a Christian become a Freemason ?

Can one be at the same time a Freemason and a Christian ?

Some years ago, Mgr. de Ketteler, Bishop of Mayence,

one of the most learned bishops and large-minded of men in Germany, was also obliged to give his attention to this subject, and he has published a pamphlet with this title : *Can a Catholic become a Freemason ?*

His answer was the same as mine: and after a careful study of the question, I must reply as he does : ' *No.*' A Catholic, a Christian, cannot be a Freemason.

Why ? Because Freemasonry is the enemy of Chris_ tianity, and in the depths of its heart an irreconcilable enemy.

I will go still further, and ask, Can a serious-minded man, a man of sound common sense, become a Freemason ?

And I must answer equally clearly, ' No.'

Then I will examine what Freemasonry is, in a social and political point of view.

But I hasten to add : it is of the *real* Freemasons that I speak, not of those numberless and honest dupes, of whom the Pope Pius IX. wrote that, in their ignorance, they went so far as to believe 'that this society is perfectly inoffensive, that it has no object but benevolence, and that it cannot in consequence be a cause of danger to the Church of God.'

Leaving the superficial part of the question alone, and that outside show which has attracted so many people to this society, my intention is to go to the bottom of things, and to find out the root from whence a radical antagonism has arisen between Freemasonry and religion, unperceived by many, but not by all, of its members.

Volumes have been written upon this institution, and volumes more may be written still. I hope to deal with the question more simply and shortly, and only study the principal points, the great lines, which decide the whole.

I shall not, therefore, occupy myself in finding out the first origin of Freemasonry, nor the successive phases of its history, nor its attitude towards different governments, nor the policy of governments as regards it. All these things may be, and are, subjects of controversy; and I only wish to speak of things which lie beyond and above all dispute.

I warn my readers also that it is not solely, but principally, of French Freemasonry that I shall speak, and perhaps also of its neighbor, Belgian Freemasonry.

The study I have made of the subject, and of which

I shall here give the results, has been from the only true source—from Freemasonry itself :

1. In the text of its constitutions and its statutes.

2. In the authentic works emanating from the different lodges.

3. In the speeches made at the most remarkable Masonic meetings.

4. In the Freemason newspapers and reviews.

5. And lastly, in its exterior and publicly declared acts.

I think, and hope, that a simple and startling light will be thrown upon the whole subject by this clear and unvarnished statement of facts.*

---

* A great many of these documents, which are absolutely incontestable, and which have in fact never been denied, are found in a very remarkable work published at Ghent by a courageous and eloquent publisher, M. A. Neut, under the title of *La Franc-Maçonnerie soumise au grand jour de la publicité, à l'aide de documents authentiques.* 2 vols. in 8vo. I have also drawn matter from the *Monde-Maçonnique*, a monthly review published by the Freemasons themselves; from the *Rituel de l'Apprenti*, by the Brother Ragon ; from the *Revue-Maçonnique* in *La Franc Maçonnerie et la Révolution*, by the P. Gautrelet, etc. ; and several other sources.

FIRST PART.

THE RADICAL ANTAGONISM BETWEEN FREEMASONRY AND RELIGION.

I.

The Position of the Question.

CAN one be at the same time a Freemason and a Christian ?

I reply, No.

Because Freemasonry, in its true spirit, in its very essence, and in its last acts, is the declared enemy of Christianity, and, by its fundamental principles, an irreconcilable enemy.

I do not mean to dwell on what may have been said or done, without any bad meaning or intention, in the different lodges, and which suffices to explain the presence of certain men, both before and after '89, who

7

were utterly blinded as to the ultimate end and object of the initiated. *Philanthropy, fraternity, humanity, progress*—all these fine words which I read at the head of the first *Revue-Maçonnique* (printed in France under the Government of July), taken in their true sense, so far from being anti-Christian, belong, on the contrary, exclusively to Christianity. It is from us that the world learnt the terms ; but the question is to know how, in reality, Freemasonry understands and practises them. The 1st article of the French Masonic Constitution, voted in 1865, declares Freemasonry to be an ' *essentially philanthropic* ' institution. It is a notable fact, however, and it is the *Monde-Maçonnique* itself which declares it, that ' Benevolence is not the *object*, but only one of the characteristics, and THE LEAST ESSENTIAL, of Freemasonry.' ' *The least essential!* ' As these gentlemen assert this, it is well not to forget it. But then the real object, the essential characteristics of the Society, I ask, what are they ? The Freemasons reply : ' The progress of humanity.' But what progress ? I reply : A pretended progress, without and against religion.

But here, at the very outset, Freemasonry stops me and exclaims : ' Religion ! Christianity ! but read my

Constitutions, then ! I don't trouble my head about them. I leave all such questions aside. I am not against Christianity. I respect the religious belief of each one of my disciples, and exclude no one for his faith. I have other things to attend to besides religion ; but I am not irreligious. To respect all religions and attack none, such will ever be the inviolable rules of Freemasonry.'

Such statements, in fact, I find incessantly in the official declarations of the Order ; and the 125th article of the Masonic Rule bears expressly on this point : 'It is a condition that in the lodges no question of religious controversy shall ever be entertained.'

But to these official declarations of Freemasonry I oppose the declarations and the speeches made in the lodges by the heads of the Order, and which have at last been published ; first in Belgium, where for a long time the lodges have enjoyed an amount of liberty which has allowed them to say everything—a liberty which they only began to enjoy in France since M. de Persigny's circular in 1864.[1] I listen then, and what do I hear ?

[1] 'Freemasonry,' says the Brother Félix Pyat, 'has been for a long while a secret society. But the time is come when she

Explosions of hatred and incessant war-cries against that very Christianity which by their constitutions they have bound themselves to *respect.*

should walk with head uplifted, and openly carry out her work. This secret society, like the ancient vestals, has constantly guarded the sacred fire, and sheltered it from the stormy winds of despotism. But to enlighten the world, the sun must come out of the cloud, the truth from behind the veil, and THE WORK FROM THE LODGE.'—*Le Rappel*, quoted by the *Masonic World* May 1870, p. 162.

II.

Declarations of the Masonic Lodges.

Christianity, it is said incessantly in the lodges, is a '*lying*' '*bastard*' 'religion,' '*repudiated by common sense,*' '*brutalizing,*' and which must be '*annihilated.*' It is a *heap of fables,*' a '*worm-eaten fabric,*' which must fall to make way for a Masonic Temple. Here are some of their formal assertions, chosen out of some thousands :

' *Catholicism is a used-up formula,* repudiated by every sensible man ; a *worm-eaten fabric !* At the end of eighteen centuries the human conscience finds itself still face to face with this *bastard religion,* propounded by the successors of the Apostles ! It is *not the lying religion of the false priests of a Christ* which will guide our steps.'[2] Thus spoke, at the installation of the Lodge of ' *Hope,*' the *great orator* of the Lodge, the Brother Lacomblé.

According to this *orator,* the ministers of the Gospel

[2] M. Neut, t i. p. 142.

11

are 'a party which has undertaken to *enchain all progress, stifle all light, and destroy all liberty*, in order to reign quietly over a *brutalized population of ignorant slaves.*'

Further on he continues : 'To-day, that the light is beginning to shine through the clouds, we must have the courage to make short work of all *this rubbish of fables*, even should the torch of reason *reduce to cinders* all that still remains standing of these *vestiges of ignorance and superstition.*' [3]

This is the way Freemasonry speaks : this is what it calls ' not troubling its head about Christianity,' and how it '*respects*' it when it does occupy its attention.

The same sentiments are expressed in all those little books with which the Revolution and Freemasonry are deluging Rome at this moment, and which I have read with my own eyes.

Its theme, its word of command, is precisely that of Voltaire : '*Let us crush the infamous one (Écrasons l'infâme).*'

These are the very words, in fact, used by the 'venerable' member of the lodge called *la Fidélité* at Ghent, on the occasion of his installation : 'In vain, with the

[3] *Ibid.*

eighteenth century, we flattered ourselves to have CRUSHED THE INFAMOUS ONE : he only takes fresh and more vigorous root. . . .'[4]

Every one knows that Freemasonry received Voltaire in its lodges, and associated its with his work. And as a further proof that, faithful to these ill-omened traditions, it has never ceased to fight with Voltaire, either privately or publicly, but with an indefatigable perseverance, against Catholic institutions and all Christian influences, we may quote the words of Brother Jean Macé, one of the most eminent of the Freemason body, who at a great Masonic dinner at Strassburg proposed the toast of Voltaire in the following words :

'To the memory of Brother Voltaire, that indefatigable soldier. All the battles he fought he gained, my brethren, on our behalf and for our profit.'[5]

According to Brother Jean Macé, *Revealed Religion* is

[4] M. Neut, t. v. p. 281.

[5] *Le Monde-Maçonnique*, May 1867, p. 25. It is a well-known fact that all the Masonic workshops of Paris, saving one, subscribed to Voltaire's statue.

a log which humanity drags after it ; but 'happily,' he adds, 'Freemasonry is at hand *to replace the faith in Revelation which is rapidly disappearing.*' [6]

Next, let us listen to the words of the Grand Master of the French Freemasons, the Brother Babaud-Laribière, nominated three years ago Prefect of the Pyrénées-Orientales, in which post he died : 'Freemasonry,' he says, 'is *superior to all dogmas.*' . . . '*Anterior and superior to all religions,*' writes another brother, '*Freemasonry is to give a new impulse to the world.*' [7] And in fact, in another speech, this very Babaud-Laribière exclaims, 'All dogmas are perishing fatally.' He therefore declares Catholic dogma dead : Rome, its capital, a dead town ; and clearly puts Freemasonry as the irreconcilable *adversary* of Catholicism : 'What is the fundamental doctrine of *our adversaries?* An immutable dogma.   What is their capital ?   A dead town.' And after this insolent assertion he goes on to proclaim Paris to be the capital of Freemasonry and the Vatican of the human race.   'Freemasonry, *on the contrary,* has established *its Vatican* here, in this Paris, where ideas

---

[6] *Le Monde-Maçonnique,* May 1870, p. 118.

[7] *Ibid.* p. 139 ; *ibid.* November 1866, p. 432.

boil and purify themselves as in a furnace.'[8] This was spoken and applauded in a general assembly of the '*Grand Orient.*'

It is Freemasonry, then, which is to *replace* Christianity. And it can do so if it will. 'WITH HER WON-DERFUL ORGANIZATION,' says F∴ Félix Pyat, 'Free-masonry MAY, IF SHE WILL, REPLACE THE CHRISTIAN CHURCH.'[9]

Such are the declarations of these gentlemen.

But we must proceed further. The hatred of Christianity becomes more and more pronounced, and arrives, if I may so speak, at its paroxysm : 'It wants energy to carry the scalpel into the very sanctuary of that blind faith *which we have sucked from our mothers' breasts.* . . . No ; THE REVEALED GOD DOES NOT EXIST.'[10]

And at Ghent, the Venerable Brother of '*La Fidélité* ' exclaims :

'We must raise ALTAR AGAINST ALTAR ; *teaching against teaching.* . . . We must fight ; but fight with the certainty of victory.'

Then he adds :

[8] *Le Monde-Maçonnique*, July 1869, p. 171.   [9] *Le Rappel*, quoted by the *Masonic World.*   [10] M. Neut, t. i. p. 144.

' To them (the ministers of Christ) we leave their *easy and* PERVERSE *morality, their gross fanaticism.* To us, pure morals, disinterestedness, self-devotion. Freemasonry rejects these idolatrous *phantasmagoria.* . . . Freemasonry is *above all religions.'* [11]

Lastly : ' We are OUR OWN GODS.' [12]

And the '*Vente Suprême*' of the Carbonarists, which has intimate affinities with Freemasonry, says frankly :

' Our final object and aim is that of Voltaire in the French Revolution : THE TOTAL ANNIHILATION FOR EVER OF CATHOLICITY AND OF ALL IDEAS OF CHRISTIANITY.' [13]

Those who fancy they can be at the same time Christians and Freemasons must begin to see that this is somewhat difficult. But Freemasonry does not restrict itself to the speeches made in its lodges ; and the warfare which it carries on against religion outside its walls is as rabid as its hatred.

[11] Speech pronounced by B. Frantz Falder on the occasion of his installation as Venerable of the Lodge of ' La Fidélité,' Ghent.—A. Neut, t. i. p. 230, *et seq.*   [12] *Ibid.*

[13] Secret Instruction addressed to all the ' *Ventes* ' by the ' *Vente Suprême,*' ' The Church in Face of the Revolution,' t. ii. p. 82.

III.

Some Examples of the War waged against Religion by Freemasonry.

Of this warfare, which is the foundation and the deepest thought of Freemasonry, I will only quote three facts, which can leave no doubt on any impartial mind as to the real spirit of the Order.

I will first ask : Was it not with a deeply-seated hostile intention that, in 1869, at Brussels, Naples, and Paris, those new councils (in Masonic language, *conventions*) were convened *in the face of the Œcumenical Council ?* And quite lately, has not a similar *'convention'* tried to meet in Rome itself ? We may remember that this Paris Convention was announced by a circular of the Grand Master of the Order, General Mellinet, who had been at the same time, under the Empire, Commander-in-chief of the National Guard of Paris.   The following is the circular :

'TT.·. CC.·. FF.·. [which means, Very dear Brothers],—The General Assembly of the " *Grand Orient* " of France, in its last Session, passed the following resolution :

'The undersigned, considering that, under present circumstances, *in the face of the Œcumenical Council which is about to open, it is important* that Freemasonry *should solemnly affirm its great principles* . . . . . etc.

'Invite the T.·. H.·. [most mighty] Grand Master and the Council of the Order to convoke, on the 8th of December next, a " *Convent* " [Convention] of the delegates of all the workshops of obedience, of those of the other rites, and of foreign lodges, to elaborate and vote *a manifesto which shall be the expression of this affirmation.*'

[The signatures follow.]

(Signed) MELLINET,

' *Grand Master of the Order.*'

I only wish to make one remark upon this circular : it is upon the motive of this projected Convention.   It is to elaborate and vote *a solemn manifesto*—for what purpose ? To affirm *certain principles* which it was *important* to lay down *in face of the Œcumenical Council.* Would it be possible to declare in a more explicit manner the flagrant antagonism between Freemasonry and the Catholic Church ? And if it were possible to have any doubt left on the subject, would it not be enough, to remove it, to remember a letter published at that time by M. Michelet, and in which the '*manifestation,*' which it was incumbent on the Freemasons to make (according to M. Michelet), 'in face of the Œcumenical Council,' would be 'THE TRUE COUNCIL WHICH WOULD JUDGE THE FALSE ONE' ? [14]

The second fact, by which the warfare declared by Freemasonry against Christianity is clearly revealed, consists in the attacks emanating from the Masonic lodges against the religious institutions of Christianity, institutions which they affirm must be '*crushed*' and 'EXTIRPATED, EVEN BY FORCE.' 'THE MONKISH HYDRA' is the term which the Venerable' of the Lodge of *The Three Friends'* applied to Christianity ; and another 'Venerable' (in a speech on the occasion of his installation), quoting this 'happy expression,' exclaims :.

[14] Letter of 24th October 1869, published in all the newspapers.

'This monkish hydra, so often crushed, threatens again to lift its hideous head ;' [15] while a third, in the midst of frantic applause, adds : 'It is our right and our duty to occupy ourselves with this question, and it is high time that the country should take the law into its own hands, EVEN SHOULD FORCE BE NECESSARY TO ERADICATE THIS LEPROSY' (bravos). [16]

And now what are we to say to those Masonic confraternities in which they enter into a formal engagement to have neither baptism, nor religious marriage, nor priest at the sick-bed ; where they go so far as to issue orders to the members of the confraternity to intervene in the most odious manner, at the last hour, between the dying man and his family, whereby the adept of Freemasonry thus deprives himself, by these sacrilegious engagements, of all possible return of conscience or repentance at the hour of death ?

From whence sprung this horrible sect, which seems to have given itself the mission to immolate all hope between what they call the 'eternal unknown' which

---

[15] M. Neut, t. i. p. 280.

[16] Speech of the Brother Bourlard at the *Grand Orient* of Belgium, June 24, 1854. Neut, t. i. p. 307.

precedes birth and the 'eternal nothingness' which follows death ? From the Masonic lodges in Belgium,
whence it passed quickly to the Masonic lodges in
France. Very soon, in fact, one of the Paris lodges
(*L'Avenir*), in imitation of the Belgian Freemasons,
created in its bosom a committee or confraternity of
this kind. The following is the 10th art. in its statutes :

'Art. 10.—Lest the free-thinker should be prevented
at the moment of death, by *strange influences*' (those of
his own family !), 'from fulfilling HIS OBLIGATIONS TO-
WARDS THE COMMITTEE, he will remit to three of the
brothers (to facilitate their mission in such a case) a
MANDATE, of which there shall be at least three official
copies, giving full authority to these brothers to *protest
loudly*, if, *for any reason whatsoever*, his formal will and
resolution should be disregarded *to be buried without any
kind of religious rite.*' [17]

And they call this the right to die in freedom (*le libre-
mourir*) ! They thus bind the will of their members.
They institute of their own free will this revolting intru-
sion in the very heart of their own families, so that these
Freemasons, armed with a threefold copy of the man-

[17] Quoted in the *Monde-Maçonnique*, t. ix.

date, may come into a house and say to the father, mother, wife, or children of the dying victim, 'This dying man, this corpse belongs to us. Be so good as to leave us alone and retire !'

It is, then, the member of the Freemason committee, and he alone, who will watch by the dying bed; and when his last hour is at hand there will be for the unhappy Freemason neither father, mother, wife, nor child; neither brother nor sister, nor any link of family or friendship or religion; nothing but the committee and its tyranny !

It is true that in France the official organ of Freemasonry has been somewhat shocked at the publicity given to this monstrous abuse, which had been but too long tolerated. From reasons of order and prudence, the Grand Master pretended that this extreme measure was a reflection on Masonic principles, and in consequence he suspended the lodge called '*L'Avenir*' for six months. But how often, and in how many other lodges and Masonic newspapers, have not the principles of the '*Avenir*' and the confraternity been proclaimed ? That which the Masonic journals, such as the *Monde-Maçonnique*, set up above everything is Atheism by the dying-

bed. These deaths without God, these departures for
eternity without any religious consolations, these fune-
rals without prayers, these are what this newspaper calls
'*dying without weakness.*' [18] In one single number I see
related and carefully chronicled five deaths and five
burials of this sort, two of which are of women ! [19] and
they are described in these terms : ' He died without the
assistance of a minister of any religion.' 'He died faithful to his principles, and was buried without a priest.'
' Useless to mention that the funeral of Mdme. F. was a
purely civil ceremony.' And again : 'Upwards of two
thousand Masons followed the hearse of Mdme. S. C.'

Elsewhere, in the same review, I read : 'Ever since
1868 Brother Bremond, treasurer of the lodge called
" *L'Echo du Grand Orient*," had entrusted to the " Venerable " of the lodge a letter, in which he declared : " I
wish to be buried *civilly and Masonically.*" ' [20]

So that I am not surprised to read in this same *Monde-
Maçonnique* that the R.∴ Lodge ' *L'Ecole Mutuelle,*' which
has for first *Sur.∴* (Inspector) Brother Tirard, placed

[18] *Le Monde-Maçonnique*, November 1856.

[19] *Ibid*. December 1867, p. 496, and September 1868, p. 80.

[20] *Ibid*. July 1873, p. 158.

among the 'orders of the day,' for discussion, the following subject :

'On the Organisation of *Civil and Masonic* Burials.' [21]

And, alas, what impieties, and, I must add, what
miserable stupidities these lodge orators indulge in on
these occasions ! Thus, at the funeral of Brother Bremond, of whom we spoke just now, Brother Pinchenat
exclaimed : 'Man dies, but his ideas do not die with
him. . . . Poor dear brother, thou wilt revive in us ! ' [22]
What a consolation for this poor Brother Bremond thus
to revive in the dear Brother Pinchenat! Do not then
talk to me any more of this toleration and respect for
religion, inscribed, must one say, so hypocritically, on
the frontispiece of the Masonic Constitution.

[21] *Ibid.* May 1866, p. 30.   [22] *Ibib,* July 1878, p. 162.

IV.

Freemasonry and the Existence of God.

But let us look at this question a little closer, and, to
show the absolute incompatibility of the fundamental
principle of Freemasonry with Christianity, let us see
how they themselves understand it, and to what a point
at last they are obliged to come : even to actual Atheism. Yes, the principle of absolute liberty of conscience,
without check or limit, which Freemasonry proclaims,
does not allow of the profession, with any consistency, I
do not say of Christianity merely, but even of belief in
the existence of God, that dogma which certain Masons
have fancied to be a primary one of their Order. In
principle, Freemasonry is a society without faith of any
sort, and without any belief, even in God. Recent debates in its body have proved this beyond doubt, even
without the imperious logic referred to above.

Let us say a few words upon these debates. An historian, a Freemason and a member at this very moment of the National Assembly, M. Henri Martin, had the misfortune to write in October 1866 the following lines in the *Siècle :*

‘Freemasonry is a Theist society, receiving into its bosom *men of every form of religion, on condition* that they profess the principle of religious liberty. Its object,’ adds M. Martin, ‘is the good of mankind and the progress of the world ; and its associates are God’s workmen towards that end. Freemasonry is either that or nothing. To wipe out from the Masonic programme *the Great Architect of the universe,* would be to blot out Freemasonry itself ; take away the Architect, and you have neither temple nor Masons. . . . The orthodox members of the Freemason body are therefore perfectly in the right when they refuse the title of Masons to those who reject the Architect and knock down His temple.’

These words roused a real storm in Freemasonry. On all sides the Masons started up with indignation at the idea that their Order should be represented as a Theist society, believing in God as the *Architect of the universe ;* and energetic protests were heard on all sides. An orator of one of the Parisian lodges, Brother Henri

Brisson, who is also a member of the National Assembly, accused M. Henri Martin of having by this statement spoken the language of 'an INTOLERANT SECTARIAN.' M. H. Martin has not understood the fundamental principle of Freemasonry. 'If to acknowledge this great Architect were,' as M. H. Martin *erroneously* asserts, 'a primary dogma of Freemasonry,' *there would be neither liberty of conscience nor freedom of opinion among the Masons.*'[23]

Two other Freemasons, who at this time were members of the Council of Order, Brother Caubet and Brother Massol (recently elected a member of the Municipal Council of Paris), declared that if Freemasonry professed faith in God, then 'Freemasonry would only be another religious sect, having, like all other sects, its dogmas, its orthodoxy, and its profession of faith.' And they quote, to support their argument, 'a report emanating from a *general commission* of Freemasons assembled in 1863, *whose conclusions were adopted.*'

This report says:

'Freemasonry is an institution *removed from all yoke of Church or priesthood, from all caprices of Revelations*

[23] *Le Temps,* November 4, 1886.

and from all the hypotheses of the mystics.'[24] The *hypotheses of the mystics,* as we too well know, signify simply the existence of God, declared many times by Brother Massol, by the partisans of moral independence, by
the Positivists, and by the Freemasons, to be ' *an hy-
pothesis which cannot be verified.'*

Thus the report adopted by the General Masonic Assembly of 1863 expressly declares that Freemasonry is
an institution freed from the yoke, not only of revealed
belief, but even of simple faith in God.

M. Henri Martin seemed, however, to have so much
the more right to represent Freemasonry as a Theist
society, that all its official documents are headed with
this formula: ' *To the glory of the Great Architect of the
universe;'* and that, still further, the question seems to
have been decided in favor of Theism in the great
Masonic Convention of 1865.

This convention had for its principal work the elabora-
tion of a new constitution for the French Masons. It
was on this occasion that the question was mooted and
discussed with renewed ardor as to whether they should
retain their old formulas for the heading of their official

acts or not. Whilst the lodge was elaborating their new constitution, out of a hundred and fifty-one motions proposed to the 'Grand Orient' at Paris, sixty of them demanded the *absolute abolition of all formulae affirming t e existence of God.*

Nevertheless, after the most animated debates in the Convention, the formula was preserved. But, alas, if the old formula remained, its logic was against it ; for it stands to reason that, logically, the abstraction of all belief proclaimed by the Masonic constitution as its fundamental basis, does not permit the obligatory prescription of a formula where the existence of God is proclaimed. In consequence, numberless protests were heard in the bosom of the lodges.

I read in the *Monde-Maçonnique :*

'In its sitting of the 26th October the first section of the great Central Lodge (Scotch rite), *composed of deputies elected by each of the lodges of their obedience,* declared that, according to their ideas, Freemasonry had no business to affirm the existence of God.' [25]

The question, therefore, was revived in the General Assembly of the 'Grand Orient,' presided over by the

---

[25] *Ibid,* November 1866, p. 413

Grand Master, General Mellinet, on the 18th June 1867. The debate was even more exciting than on the previous occasion. 'On this question,' writes the *Monde-Maçon- nique*, 'hangs the very existence of Freemasonry, that which constitutes its *raison d'être*, and which is as the marrow of its bones.'[26] 'They say,' exclaims the same journal with indignation, 'we are Deists: Freemasonry is the eldest daughter of Deism.' Will Freemasons agree to this proposition? We will see if they are willing to COVER THEMSELVES WITH SHAME; they who have proclaimed so loudly their UNIVERSAL TOLERA- TION![27]

We have before us the curious debates which took place in that General Masonic Assembly, which con- sisted of '260 delegates, representing 183 workshops.' The adversaries of the formula maintained that Free- masonry should give a definition of God, or not speak of it any more, for to admit all the gods would be a ne- gation; that 'morality does not need to lean upon God;' and that 'Freemasonry, by affirming the idea of God, would pass into the condition of a Church.'[28]

[26] April 1867. p. 50.   [27] August 1866, p. 220.

[28] *Ibid.* July 1867

Notwithstanding this logic, the tactics of prudence won the day. The formula was retained. But, in reality, what did this vote mean ?   And to those who understand what Freemasonry really means, can anything be more empty ? Annulled by Masonic toleration, which, *admitting all the gods, is but a negation*—that is to say, Atheism, according to the frank expression of Brother Pelletan—can this formula be taken seriously ? 'Is it not true,' exclaimed another brother, Brother Garisson, at the Masonic Convention—'is it not true that Proudhon, one of the master-minds of this century, has been received among the Freemasons ? Have not the young men of the Liége Congress been received ? Yes, certainly. We have stretched out to them the hand of fellowship, and have said to them : *Work with us !* ' (Applause.)[29]

Yes, all this is quite true. Yes. Proudhon was received as a Freemason—the man who said, ' God is the origin of evil ; ' and who to the question, ' What do we owe to God ? ' replied, ' *War.*'

And the young men of the Liége Congress, who uttered those horrible and savage cries 'Hatred to God !'

[29] *Ibid.*

'War to God!' 'We will rend the heavens like a sheet of paper!'—these young men were considered admirable auxiliaries to Freemasonry, which has stretched out to them the hand of fellowship. In truth, those among the Freemasons who had any logical consequence have never ceased to protest against this formula, and hope soon to arrive at making it disappear from the regulations. 'Our contradictors,' writes the *Monde-Maçonnique* (in the same number in which the vote was recorded), 'have only acquired the right to be intolerant;' and Freemasonry remains 'the universal temple eternally opened TO ATHEISTS as well as *to Pantheists*,' etc. etc.[30]

And if we wish to learn what is hidden under this formula, even for those who adopt it, it is the annihilation of all forms of worship. Read in the *Ritual for the Mason Apprentice* the commentary given by the 'Venerable' to the neophyte about to be received :

'Deism is belief in God *without revelation* or *form of worship*. It is the religion of the future, *destined to replace all religions*,' etc.[31]

[30] *Ibid.* July 1867.   [31] *Ritual of the Mason Apprentice*, containing the Ceremonial, by J. M. Rago , p. 45.

Listen, again, to the peremptory professions of faith made in the great Masonic assemblies :

' I affirm that THE NAME OF GOD IS A WORD VOID OF SENSE.' [32]

' We must not only place ourselves above different religions, BUT ABOVE ALL BELIEF IN ANY GOD WHATEVER.' [33]

' It is ONLY FOOLS WHO SPEAK AND DREAM STILL OF A GOD.' [34]

Thus we have a Deist etiquette which is, at bottom, nothing but a declaration of open war against all positive religion ; this very etiquette repudiated as strongly by the most active and working members of the association as by logical principles ; a total abstraction of all dogma, the principle of absolute and unrestrained liberty —that is to say, absolute indifferentism—consecrating a negation of the most audacious kind, and carrying away, little by little, the last remains of a worn-out formula ; the most nihilist doctrines invading the lodges more and more, and Atheism proclaiming itself, and installing itself, if I may venture to say so, with supreme audacity

[32] *Liège Lodge.* 865. A. Neut, xi. p. 287.

[33] *Ibid.* p. 223.   [8] *Ibid.*

on the ruins of all belief in God.   Such is, at this very moment, the doctrinal schedule of Freemasonry.

Can any one seriously, after this, put the question if a Christian can be a Freemason ?

V.

Freemasonry and the Immortality of the Soul.

As regards the immortality of the soul, the same debates arose in the bosom of Freemasonry as those on the
belief in God.

Thus when the last king of the Belgians died, Leo-
pold—although he received the consolations of the Protestant faith, and in consequence really abjured Freemasonry—the Belgian Freemasons were determined to take
possession of his memory, and a great funeral ceremony
was celebrated in his honor at the 'Grand Orient' in
Belgium. But the following words had been attached
to the rood-loft of the Masonic Temple by the directors
of the ceremony :

'*The soul, emanating from God, is eternal.*'

Against which monstrous (?) assertion the Louvain
Lodge, '*La Constance,*' addressed the following protest
to the 'Grand Orient :'

'Considering that *free-thinking* has been admitted by

the Belgian lodges *as a fundamental principle*, the lodge the " Constance," the " Orient " of Louvain, energetically protests against this blow dealt by the "Grand Orient" to the principles which are the basis of Freemasonry.' [35]

This protest of the Freemasons of ·Louvain was warmly applauded in England and France. A Masonic journal, the *Chain of Union*, from London, wrote :

Who can affirm that the soul, emanating from God, is immortal ? Who has any proof of it ? For centuries Popes and Councils have sought for this evidence and have not found it, . . . and they will never find it in heaven, because the HUMAN SOUL IS SELF CREATED.

' We support, therefore, the protest of our brothers of Louvain. It is with such phrases, always empty and incoherent, and emanating from the region of fancy and imagination, that one arrives, sooner or later, at enslaving (*encapuciner*) a country. Brothers of Louvain, you were right to protest.' [36]

[35] *Protestation of the Lodge ' Constance' of Louvain.* Dated 17th day, first month, 5866 (1866). Quoted by M. Nent.

[36] The *Chain of Union.* London, 1st May 1866. Quoted by the *Monde-Maçonnique.*

And on their side the *Monde-Maçonnique* exclaims :

' How is it that the Belgian Grand Orient does not understand that, by publicly affirming through this inscription the immortality of the soul, a serious attack is made on liberty of conscience ? ' [87]

The ' Grand Orient' in consequence spurned the protest—but how ? Was it by affirming the immortality of the soul ? *No ;* it declared the formula was not used in a serious sense ; that it compelled no one to believe in it ; and was only admitted on that occasion out of respect to old traditions ; that these questions of God and the soul cannot possibly receive *any real solution ;* and that, in fact, the essence of Freemasonry was not to profess any form of belief.

' Already, in 1837, the " Grand Orient" of Belgiun, had freed national Freemasonry from all religious and philosophic dogmas. . . . The " Grand Orient" prescribes no dogma whatever. If the principle of the immortality of the soul should appear in its rituals or in its formularies, if the idea of God should be produced under the denomination of the " Great Architect of the

---

[87] The *Monde-Maçonnique*, November 1866. p. 421.

universe," *it is because such are the traditions of the Order.*
But this formula is binding on no man's conscience.   In
these days it would be puerile to strive to raise questions
which *can lead to no possible solution !* '

And to show still more clearly what this unbelief al-
lows the lodges to say, I will quote a few more fragments
of speeches made at the funeral of certain brothers who
had objected to receiving the consolations of religion on
their death-beds :

' In the supreme recollection of his conscience he advanced towards the infinite with the calm of antiquity.'
This is spoken of a Freemason who died as he had lived,
without Christ and without God.   ' A *true Mason* ought
to die as he had lived, as a *free-thinker*, and so far from
looking upon such a death *as a disgrace*, it is a title
which should be frankly claimed. . . .' [38]

We have numberless Masonic speeches before our
eyes where the same language has been held.   What
does Brother Ragon (the founder of the lodge of the
' *Trinosophes* ' at Paris, and the author of the ritual we
have lately quoted) think of death and immortality ?

[38] Speech of Brother Ranwet, Sov. Gr. Commander.   Neut, t. 1.
p. 155.

That death is nothing but 'the DEPERSONIFICATION of the individual, whose material elements,' continues Brother Ragon (and this is *immortality* as he understands it), 'are decomposed, united to analogous elements, and thus concur in the infinite transformations of continually-animated matter."

Certainly it would be impossible to profess more crudely a coarser Materialism or a more barefaced Atheism.

And what shall we say of that curious funeral oration pronounced over the tomb of Brother Bourdet (of the R. L. '*La Persévérance*' of the O ∴ of Arles) by Brother Coindre ? 'Brother Bourdet, each of the parts of thy body is about to disappear from us, and return to the *universal crucible* whence they came out, to concur in the formation of *a myriad* of other bodies.' [39]

So Brother Bourdet has made great progress. But his soul—where is it going ? Of his soul, as a matter of course, not one word. Masonic immortality, in the theories which we have just enunciated, consists neither in the immortality of the soul nor of the person, because, on the contrary, the individual is '*depersonified*' by

[39] *Le Monde-Maçonnique*, July 1867, p. 173.

death ; but in that of the material elements, which have
not been annihilated.   It is the same with his ideas :
' *The idea which the dead man followed will not die with
him ; it passes into the mind of those who remain,*' and
(they add gravely) ' IN SUCH A WAY THAT NOTHING IS
LOST. . . .'

Is not this hiding, under a laughable and lying formula, the most miserable hopes ?

Elsewhere, on the tomb of the Head of the 'Grand
Orient' of Belgium, Brother Verhagen exclaims : ' He
did not allow his last moments to be preceded by *superstitious expiations.*'

These are the terms in which Freemasons speak of
the consolations which religion, and religion alone, can
give to the dying, at that terrible moment when the
world vanishes from their gaze, to leave them alone
with an eternal future.   The orator continues : ' Our
regrets are not troubled by *vain fears*, our hopes do not
rest *on ideas of vain credulity.* . . . Certain *emblematic
purifications* warn us that the *creating fire* is the *sole
purificator* of nature.' [40]

The orator, in fact, exposed this beautiful theory of

[40] M. Neut, t. i. p. 149.

the *creating fire* and *sole purificator of nature* before a monument, at the foot of which rose a cypress. In front of the platform, on an altar of a cubic form, were placed vases of silver and crystal, containing *fire, incense or perfume, lustral water*, etc. Fire, perfumes, lustral water—it is, as one can see, a complete worship —nothing is wanting. And in all the accounts of the funeral ceremonies which the Freemasons celebrate amongst themselves in their temples, what a strange ceremonial ! And at the bottom of it all, what emptiness ! Grand-sounding words covering such empty ideas ! What pomp in nothingness !

I copy literally a Masonic *tracé ;* that is to say, an official report. It is upon the last honors paid to Brother Fontainas, Burgomaster of Brussels :

When the Supreme Council has taken the place reserved for it, the Venerable Master in the chair recollects himself, and says :

'First Brother Superintendent, what o'clock is it ?'

The *F.B.S.:* 'The hour when the end has become the beginning.'

The *Venerable Master* in the chair : 'It is the law of

nature.' (A great truth, certainly !) 'My brothers, let us do our duty.'

He then walks, followed by the Supreme Council, the deputies of the different lodges, and the Brothers who are to decorate the columns, to the tomb.

The *Venerable Master* in the chair : 'Brother Andrew Fontainas, answer us !'

In vain the First and Second Brothers Superintendents repeat the same mournful appeal. The tomb remains dumb. The Venerable then says : 'The Master remains deaf to the voice of his Brothers.' I should think so ! He has been already buried for several days.

These words are followed by the lugubrious sounds of the tum-tum, the vibration of which expires slowly under the roof of the temple.

The Brother orator then pronounces a 'bit of architecture' (in other words, a speech). I quoted a portion of it above : 'A true Mason should die as he has lived,' etc.

Then, after the ceremonies (which I have abridged), they go to the *temple of immortality,* which is all lit up with burning torches. There another Brother orator explains what are the Masonic hopes, freed, let it be clearly understood, 'from all the prisons of Catholic dogma and other particular sects.'

The *Monde-Maçonnique* was thus quite right to designate in this manner the two pompous formulas of Freemasonry : '*God, the Great Architect of the universe*,' 'a generic denomination which all the world may accept, EVEN THOSE WHO DO NOT BELIEVE IN GOD.'

'*The immortality of the soul*,' or the perpetuity of *existence*, if NOT INDIVIDUAL, AT LEAST COLLECTIVE ;[41] that is, not the immortality of the soul and of the individual, but the perpetuity of the species. So that Brother Dr. Guépin could say without being contradicted :

'The majority, which has chosen to inscribe over our sanctuaries God and the immortality of the soul, is intolerant.' And the pastor Zille, whom I quoted just now, added : 'Only FOOLS, ignorant and weak in understanding, dream still of God and of the IMMORTALITY OF THE SOUL.'

[41] *Le Monde-Maçonnique*, t. iv. p. 657.

VI.

*Incompatibility of the Fundamental Principle of Freema-
sonry with all Religion.*

It is thus evident, if we choose to reflect for a moment,
that the fundamental principle of Freemasonry implies,
not only a formal negation of Christianity, but, besides,
a flagrant philosophical error. It is a very formula of
scepticism and of the most complete indifferentism.

What, in fact, is the principle? Free-thinking.
'Free-thinking is the FUNDAMENTAL PRINCIPLE of Freemasonry'[42] 'Not RESTRAINED, but COMPLETE[43] and universal liberty.' 'A liberty which shall be ABSOLUTE,
without limit, *in its fullest extent.*'[44] 'Absolute liberty
of conscience is the ONLY BASIS of Freemasonry.'[45]
'Freemasonry is, in fact, ABOVE all dogmas.'[46] It is

[42] A. Neut, t. 1. 408.

[43] *Le Monde-Maçonnique*, November 1866, p. 441.

[44] *Ibid*, May 1866, p. 22.   [45] *Ibid.*   [46] *Ibid*

44

'ABOVE all religions.'[47] 'Liberty of conscience is SUPE-
RIOR TO ALL FORMS of religious belief'[48] (whatever they
may be, even to the belief in God). 'Freemasonry is
an institution withdrawn from all the HYPOTHESES OF
THE MYSTICS.'[49] 'Freemasons ought, in consequence, to
place themselves, not only above different religions, but
entirely above all belief IN ANY GOD WHATSOEVER.'[50]
Finally, they go so far as to say : 'We will be our *own
priests* and our OWN GODS.[51] And this unlimited, complete, and universal liberty is a RIGHT.'[52] Thus liberty,
right—not in regard to the civil law, but to the interior
conscience—liberty, the absolute universal right to believe what one wills, as one wills, or not to believe anything at all—this *right*, which is proclaimed to be anterior and superior to all religious convictions or forms
of belief—this is the fundamental principle (according
to the Freemasons themselves) and the sole basis of
Freemasonry.

Well, it is manifest from the very first, that this prin-

---

[47] M. Neut, t i. p. 200.   [48] *Ibid*, t ii. p. 192.

[49] *Le Monde Maçonnique*, November 1866, p. 441.

[50] M. Neut, t. ii. p. 233   [51] *Ibid*. p. 202.

[52] *Constitution Maçonnique*. Art. L

ciple, understood in this manner, is a flagrant philosophical error; and, I beg pardon of those gentlemen
Freemasons who believe in God, it is the implicit negation even of natural religion.

In truth, where natural religion exists, it *obliges* by itself, in principle and right; this obligation is *anterior*
and *superior* to man; it *limits* his liberty; it *binds* his
conscience. In the face of this obligation man may find
an *excuse* for unbelief in his ignorance or good faith;
but not a *right anterior* and *superior* to the law. This
is the equivocation and the capital error of the Masonic
principle. Certainly it is not sufficient to name one's
conscience in order to have the *right* to do what one
wills, and to deny everything.

And to demonstrate this by a striking example, it is
not enough, as M. Laboulaye said very forcibly on the
subject of the Mormons—it is not enough (to free oneself
from all obligations) to be able to say, 'My conscience
exacts that I should take several wives.' No; that is
not enough, neither in the face of morality nor of the
civil law.

This identical reasoning may be applied to Christianity. If it be a divine institution, it *obliges* all men by it-

self ; and this *obligation*, superior to the individual (un-
less one proclaims the individual to be superior to God),
limits his liberty. There, again, ignorance or good faith
may plead an *excuse*, but not create an absolute unlimited right, *anterior* and *superior* to Christianity.

This absolute and unlimited liberty of conscience
which Freemasons claim as the basis of Freemasonry
does not, therefore, exist. It is one of those chimeras of
false liberalism condemned by the Church, and is
nothing else than scepticism and indifferentism in the
matter of faith. To proclaim it, as Freemasonry does,
is to deny implicitly, but really, all natural and revealed
religion.

The Masonic principle is, therefore, exclusive of
Christianity ; and hence a Christian cannot be a Freemason.

Besides all this, when an institution or society pro-
poses to itself, like Freemasonry, to carry out the progress, not only material, but intellectual and moral, of
humanity, outside the pale of religion and Christianity,
what does it do but offer itself as a substitute for every
kind of religion, and consequently deny it ? For if
Christianity be useless or superfluous for such work,

men need have nothing to do with it ; it is meant for
that, or it is worth nothing.

When, then, the *Monde-Maçonnique* comes and tells us
that the province of Freemasonry is to include all men,
no matter to what religion they belong, I beg its pardon
again ; but the *Monde-Maçonnique* does not understand
itself ; and little as men may be disposed to go to the
bottom of things, they must see that to lay down such
principles as the basis of the Masonic constitutions, and
then to pretend that they do not touch the question of
religion, is a simple contradiction, if not a cheat.

This is what a high dignitary of one of the German
lodges avowed, with a frankness which leaves nothing
to be desired :

'Freemasonry and Catholicism,' he writes, 'recipro-
cally exclude each other : THEY ARE THE ANTIPODES. . . .
I ask how a Catholic can remain faithful to his religion
all the while professing Freemason principles. . . . A
man who believes in the symbol of the Apostles, how
can he allow that he is *free* and not *bound to any religious
belief?* These things are direct contradictions.'—Extract from pamphlet, *Vio gegenwart und Zukunft der
Praimaurerei in Deutschland* (Leipzig, 1854), p. 116.

VII.

Fresh Details as to the Warfare declared against Christianity—Morality without God—Education without religion.

Freemasonry is, then, a serious war declared against all religion. But the odious object of the Freemasons appears specially in the zeal they show in preaching morality without God, and in consequence, in separating the instruction of youth from all religious belief.

Morality, they declare, is the essence of Freemasonry; but this morality they are determined shall be without Christianity. In the lodges were conceived, and from the lodges emanated, that impious chimera which they call '*independent morality*,' and which is only another form of Atheism.

In one sense, however, it is far from being a chimera, but a fact, which the Paris 'Commune,' when triumphant, hastened to realize by turning out of the schools all religious emblems or instruction; and even recently, coming back to the traditions of the Commune, the General Council voted in the same sense and with the same intention obligatory *secular* education.

' *Morality independent of all religious hypotheses,*' [53] such is the axiom of Freemasonry ; and the conclusion they draw from it is this : that all religious instruction *should be suppressed*, and the reason they allege is, that religious belief is useless for the young ; and, still more, that ' *Faith in God takes away the dignity of man, troubles his reason, and may lead him to the abandonment of all morality.*' This has been expressly declared in the .ᴿ.˙. L.˙. *La Rose du parfait Silence*, in Paris. To this question, in fact, ' Should religious education be suppressed ?' the answer was, ' *Without any doubt*' ; and the orator of the R.˙. L.˙. developed his answer in these terms : ' *The principle of a supernatural authority*, that is to say, faith in God, *takes away the dignity of man*, and is even *likely to lead him to the abandonment of all morality.*' . . . ' The respect we owe specially to the mind of a child,' he adds, ' forbids us to inculcate doctrines *which might trouble his reason.*' [54]

[53] *Le Monde-Maçonnique*, May 1867, p. 51.]

[54] *Ibid*. October 1866, pp. 372, 373.

Do we wish for another witness ? I read again the following passage in the *Monde-Maçonnique :* [55] ' The R ∴. Lodge, called the "*Amie de l'Ordre*," Orient of Paris, has lately propounded the following question : " *What kind of education should a Mason give to his children ?* " '

" All the orators declared themselves partisans of a liberal and *secular* education, independent of *narrow-minded religious instruction.*'

And the *Monde-Maçonnique* quotes another of these speeches in its entirety ; of which I will only give the following extract :

' Do not let us hear any more of that *bastard, false education, based on superannuated dogmas.* . . . This method of bringing up our children has lasted too long: *it is time, high time, that it should come to an end.* . . . The basis on which the education of our children should rest is this : " Let us teach them to admire and study the phenomena of nature," ' . . . and the orator adds, ' without troubling our heads as to the name with which we should adorn these fine things." [56]

[55] T. xiii. May 1870, p. 10.

[56] *Le Monde-Maçonnique,* t xiii. pp. 14, 15.

But here is a more paternal sentiment still, which is, we suppose, to inspire these gentlemen in the education of their children:

'Freemasonry,' says Brother Massol, in one of the sittings of the Masonic *International* Session held in July 1867, 'ought to be, and is, only a school of morality, *independent of all religious dogmas. . . .* I have myself brought up children, but I have never lied to them. Each time that they have asked me, "What was meant by God?" I have answered, "I KNOW NOTHING ABOUT IT." *It is thus I have acted with men.*'[57]

Let us see, further, how a piece of Masonic poetry of Brother Lachambaudie, read at a Masonic banquet, treats the Christian Catechism :

> ' Quel est-ce livre élémentaire ?
> Des superstitions, où la raison s'altère ;
> C'est un tissu. . . .'[58]

(What is this elementary book ? Superstitions, where reason is debased ; a tissue . . .)

The Belgian lodges were determined not to be outdone in this particular by the French ones. Thus, in 1864,

[57] *Le Monde-Maçonnique,* August 1867, pp. 196, 197.

[58] *Ibid.* April 1867, p. 722.

the *Grand Orient* of Belgium—you see, I do not quote minor Masonic authorities—put the same question among the *orders of the day* to all the Lodges of Obedience. The lodges answered—and we shall see to what lengths the Antwerp Lodge, in particular, did not fear to go in its reply—'THE TEACHING OF THE CATECHISM IS THE GREATEST OBSTACLE TO THE DEVELOPMENT OF A CHILD'S FACULTIES. THE INTERVENTION OF A PRIEST in education DEPRIVES THE CHILDREN OF ALL MORAL, *logical, and rational teaching.*' [59]

From the different answers sent by the Lodges of Obedience to the *Grand Orient* of Belgium came forth a project of a New Law, in 23 Arts., of which the first article was entitled, 'SUPPRESSION OF ALL RELIGIOUS EDUCATION;' and the second, 'OBLIGATION FOR A FATHER OR A WIDOWED MOTHER to FORCE *their children to school.*'

Remark the formidable connection between these two articles. According to them, if the wishes of these great Liberals be fulfilled, the law will FORCE the father, the mother, or the widow, to drag their children to a

[59] *Journal de Bruxelles*, 28th November 1864. Quoted by M. Neut, t. l. p. 147.

school where all religious education will be suppressed. And therefore it is that, both at Paris and Brussels, they claim so ardently lay, free, and obligatory education. 'On this question, all the efforts of Freemasonry,' [60] says the *Monde-Maçonnique*, 'should be concentrated.' And why ? The Belgian lodges have not dissimulated the answer. In order that children should be brought up— 'BY FORCE '—without God and without any religious teaching.

And the *Chain of Union*, the Masonic journal in London, answering the Antwerp lodge and the Belgian *Grand Orient*, and the *Rose du parfait Silence* at Paris, gave the real reason : it declared that religious education was a poison, and demanded in consequence, 'that parents should BIND THEMSELVES BY PROMISE *to withdraw their children from the* VIRUS *of* religious *education.'* [61]

Thus the child is *no longer to belong to its parents*, and the law will FORCE them to send their little ones to schools from whence all knowledge of God and all religious teaching shall be excluded.

[60] The *Monde-Maçonnique*, October 1866, p. 858.

[61] *Ibid*. 1st May 1865,

Certainly, if there be an odious and execrable tyranny it is this one. Also, M. Ledru Rollin one day expressed himself on the subject in the following energetic words : ' Can there be a greater suffering for an individual than the forcible deportation of his son into a school which he looks upon as a place of perdition ? Can there be a greater tyranny than this conscription of infancy, violently dragged into the enemy's camp, and to serve that very enemy ? ' [62]

Well, it is on this very capital point—I cannot repeat it too often—this point of *obligatory and atheistical education*, that Freemasonry in Belgium and France is at this moment putting forth its greatest efforts. The *Monde-Maçonnique* declared it just now, and elsewhere also it exclaimed : ' An immense field is open to our activity. Ignorance and superstition weigh heavily upon the world. Let us create *schools, professional chairs, libraries.'*

Besides all this (for MM. the Freemasons are men who act at the same time that they talk), Freemasonry ' *adopts*,' as it calls it, a large number of children ; and I

[62] Spoken at the Corps Législatif, and quoted by M. Neut, t. 1. p. 350.

am not, in consequence, surprised to read, in the *procés-verbal* of the ‘ *International Masonic Protectorate,*’ which, on the 27th July 1867, closed its session organized by the Scotch lodges, the following words :

‘ Seventy-nine children, *the greater part of whom were girls,* came, accompanied by their families, to ask protection and shelter of Freemasonry ; seventy-nine children whose intelligence will not be POISONED by *retrograde theories;* seventy-nine children, MOSTLY GIRLS, who will *sow our ideas* in the fertile field of the future.’

On the other hand, the Masonic *Convent* of 1870 *unanimously adopted* the following decision : [63]

‘French Freemasonry will associate itself with the efforts made in other countries to compel the establishment of free, compulsory, and SECULAR education.’,[64] *Secular :* not only imparted by seculars, but separated from all religion.[65] ‘ Every one knows ’ (adds the *Monde-*

---

[63] The *Monde-Maçonnique,* t. x. p. 267.   [64] *Ibid.* May 1870, p. 202.

[65] This is a matter which was not very clearly understood by an honest laborer, of whom the following story was told me the other day : ‘ I wish,’ said he to the Christian Brothers, bringing them one day his little boy, ‘ that my son should receive a secular education.’ ‘ But then,’ replied the Brothers, ‘ it is not to us that you must

Maçonnique) 'that this decision was sent to M. Jules Simon, in order that he might support it in the Legislative Assembly.'

In the same way in Belgium, at the great 'National Solstitial' feast celebrated at Brussels, Brother Boulard exclaimed : 'When ministers come forward to announce to the country how they intend to organize the new scheme of popular education, I will exclaim : "To me, as a Freemason, to me belongs the education question ! It is for me to examine, for me to discover the solution !" (cheers).' [66] And this impious proselytism has been solemnly practised in Belgium and France. At Brussels, on the 10th October 1865, on the occasion of the inauguration of a statue erected in honor of the Great Master of Belgian Freemasonry, M. Verhaegen, the Freemasons had the audacity to send for the children of the National Schools, and to make them sing the following atheistic verses :

confide him.' 'O yes,' rep lied the good workman ; 'I want my boy to receive a secular education, *as I was told at the Municipal Council.* But, all the same, I choose that he should be brought up, like me, by the Brothers.'

LE CHŒUR.

Ouvrez, ouvrez toutes les portes,

Le monument s'est élargi,

Pour laisser entrer les cohortes

De *l'enseignement affranchi.*

PREMIER GROUPE.

Ce temple d'intelligence,

Marque au progrès une ère **immense,**

Quel est son temple ?

SECOND GROUPE.

La Science.

PREMIER GROUPE.

Quel est son Dieu?

SECOND GROUPE.

La Liberté.

Plus de dogme—aveugle lien !

Plus de jougs, tyrans, *ni Messies !*

CHŒUR GENERAL.

Elève et maître, il fant qu'ensemble nous dotions

De mâles générations

Les prochaines démocraties.[67]

[67] Quoted by M. Neut, t. l. p. 362.

[TRANSLATION.

The Choir : Open, open all the doors. The monument is enlarged, to let in the troops of free education.

First Group : This temple of knowledge marks a new era. What is its temple ?

Second Group : Science.

First Group : What is its God ?

Second Group : Liberty. No more dogmas, *blind bondage !* No more *yokes, tyrants, or Messiahs !*

General Choir : Masters and scholars, together let us endow manly generations of *future democrats.*]

These doctrines, alas ! every day make more and more way ; and at Paris, during the Commune, with which, as we have already seen, Freemasonry showed such strange sympathies, did they not compel a child of twelve years old to go up into the pulpit at St. Sulpice and proclaim, amidst the fearful applause of a mad populace, that there was no God ?

VIII.

*Propaganda of Education without Religion in Adult Schools
—Professional College for Girls—The Education League.*

Freemasonry displays the same proselytizing ardor
to get possession of adults for their atheistical teaching.
Thus the Masonic orator who, in the Lodge of the ' *Rose
du parfait Silence,*' at Paris, declared that ' religious
education was useless for the discipline of children, and
likely to lead them to the abandonment of all morality,'
wound up his speech in these terms : 'I breathe an
ardent wish that eloquent Masons could be found who
should devote themselves to setting up classes for teaching elementary science and universal morality to the
workmen in all the towns of France.' Without a question, of course, of that *religious teaching* which would
be likely to induce them *to give up morality !* [68]

Certainly it is high time that we Catholics should be
inspired with as much zeal to enlighten the working

[68] *Le Monde Maçonnique,* October 1866, p. 374.

classes as the Freemasons have to corrupt them. But the especial object,and aim of these Freemasons is to pervert women. Yes, this terrible conspiracy, which attempts to drag the Faith from the hearts of wives, mothers, and daughters, who are its indefatigable promoters ? The Freemasons.

Let us listen to what Brother Massol says on this subject, in the Lodge of ' *Bienfaisance et Progrès*,' at Boulogne, on the 19th of July 1867 :

'By proper teaching, *women* will at last arrive at shaking off *the yoke of the clergy*, and freeing themselves from *superstitions* which prevent their receiving an education corresponding with the requirements of modern opinion. To give a proof of this, where is the English, American, or German woman who, to the two questions which their children might ask them, "Who has created the world ? " and " Do we exist after death ?" would dare to answer that she does not know, and that "no one knows anything about it ? " Well, this courage a well-taught Frenchwoman would have.' [69]

Is that quite clear ?

And the reason of this propaganda Brother **Albert**

[69] *Le Monde-Maçonnique*, August 1867, p. 205.

Leroy (formerly professor of rhetoric, if I am not mistaken, at the Versailles Lyceum, under the Ministry of M. Jules Simon) clearly demonstrated in these terms, in a Masonic International Session held in the month of August 1837, at Paris : ' Without women all the men together will never be able to succeed.' [70]

Two contemporary and startling facts besides bear witness to this activity on the part of the Freemasons to propagate atheistical instruction without any religion. I speak of the creation of *Professional Schools for Girls* and of the *Education League.*

The Professional School for Girls.—Under the Empire, in a pamphlet which I called *Les Alarmes de l'Episcopat,* and to which almost all the bishops of France gave in their adhesion by publicly-printed letters, I denounced this institution as one of the most dangerous kind. I proved that the thoughts whence these schools emanated were of the most anti-Christian and anti-religious character ; that, under pretence of secular instruction, it was in reality practical irreligion which they were striving to inculcate in the minds of those young girls ; that they deliberately proposed to make free-thinkers

[70] *Le Monde-Maçonnique,* August 1867.

of them, so as to induce them to live and die without any sort of Christianity or religion. Not a word which I then stated has ever been or could ever be denied or contradicted. I quoted, in fact, the declarations of the founders themselves, and the too striking example of their lives and their deaths ; the impious speeches made over their tombs in presence of their pupils ; the formal terms of their official prospectus. In a word, I proved peremptorily that this institution had two faces : one on which was inscribed, for the sake of their dupes, ' *Professional Teaching* '—that was their ensign ; the other on which might have been inscribed, ' *No more Christianity, neither in life nor death* '—that is their real object and aim. What I now add here is, that Freemasonry had the main part in this work ; that the most ardent propagators of these schools were Freemasons and their newspapers. Everything, in fact, about these schools was Masonic ; the object, namely, education without religion, or practical irreligion ; and the means, the great means, employed by the Masonic propaganda, *i.e.* schools, teaching, perversion of young girls and of women by so-called secular, *i.e.* anti-Christian, education.

But still more formidable than these professional

schools, because its diffusion, thanks to the frivolity and indifference of the public mind, has been rapid and universal in our country, is the *League* called of *Education*, founded in Belgium by Freemasons, and imported from Belgium into France by a celebrated Freemason whom I have already quoted, Brother Jean Macé.

It was, in fact, as one may read in the *Second Bulletin of the League*, after having assisted at Liége at a session of the 'Belgian Education League,' that Brother Jean Macé resolved 'to induce the French to form an analogous League.'

This Masonic origin of the League reveals its object clearly enough. And as to Brother Jean Macé himself, to know the spirit which inspired him, we need only refer to his toast on the occasion of the inauguration of a new Masonic lodge at Strassburg : 'To the memory of Brother Voltaire,'[71] etc. . . . Like the professional school for girls, the Education League has two objects—one proclaimed and one hidden. The avowed object is the diffusion of education. But what education ? That is what they do not state, except to their adepts : education without God, independent of all religion, and the

[71] The *Monde-Maçonnique*, May 1867, p. 252.

result of which is to bring up men to live and die as if Christianity had never existed. This is the real object of the League.

If a number of careless or deceived persons have entered into this League, without a thought of looking further than to the outward sign, let them listen to what the Freemason press (which knows very well what it says and does) have written on this subject :

' We are happy to announce,' writes the *Monde-Maçonnique*, in its April number (1837), 'that the subscriptions for THE EDUCATION LEAGUE AND THE STATUE OF BROTHER VOLTAIRE meet with the warmest sympathy IN ALL OUR LODGES. It would be impossible to have two subscriptions more in harmony with each other : ' Voltaire, that is to say, the destruction of *all prejudices and superstitions*' (translate *religions*), 'and the *Education League*, that is to say, the building up of a new society, based on science and instruction ALONE' (that is, free from every kind of religion). 'ALL OUR BROTHERS UNDERSTAND IT THUS.' And again, a little further on : ' *The principles* which we profess are *in entire unison* WITH THOSE WHICH INSPIRED THE PROJECT OF BROTHER JEAN MACÉ.'

Remember, it is the *Monde-Maçonnique* which writes
this—a newspaper which, in all its pages, declares that
all religions are darkness ; that Freemasonry is light ;
that God, the soul, and a future life are only hypotheses,
phantoms ; that, in consequence, man should be edu-
cated and his progress realized above and outside all
Christianity and all religion.   And this newspaper declares that *its principles are in perfect unison* with those
which inspired the PROJECT of the League of Brother
Jean Macé, and which adds : ' Freemasons should ad-
here *in a body* (*en masse*) to the Education League, and
the lodges should study, in the peaceful deliberations of
their temples, how to make it more EFFICACIOUS.'

This is, after all, what Brother Jean Macé acknowledged in another toast : '*To the alliance of the League
and Freemasonry,*' and in which he declared that all Freemasons should be leaguers, and all leaguers Freemasons ;
*that the object, principle, and aim of the League and Free-
masonry were identical ;* and he gave the following
toasts :

1. To the entry of all Freemasons into the League.

2. To the entry into Freemasonry of all members of
the League.

3. To the triumph of the light—the *mot d'ordre* common to both the League and Freemasonry !'[72]

And this appeal was so well responded to that, in a *Report of the First Year of the Propagation of the League in France*, Brother Jean Macé boasted that all the French departments, save twelve, were enrolled in the League ; ' and thus,' he adds, 'the French League will end by becoming a GREAT ARMY.' An educational army, certainly, which no minister of public instruction will easily govern.

Before such evidence of facts and principles, in the face of such ends and objects and of such a propaganda, whatever may be the contrary feelings of a few deceived members of Freemasonry or of a few less advanced lodges, is there any occasion to discuss the question further in order to decide if a Christian or a Catholic can belong to such a society or be associated with such a work ? No ; such a solidarity is impossible. And the author of the *History of Freemasonry*, Brother Goffin, proclaimed it honestly and frankly :

'When Freemasonry admits into its temples a Jew, a Mahometan, a Catholic, or a Protestant, it is on con-

[72] The *Monde-Maçonnique*, July 1869.

dition that the postulant shall become a new man ; that
he shall abjure his past errors, and lay down the superstitions in which he has been cradled from his youth.
Without that, what business has he in our Masonic assemblies ? ' [73]

What could I say that was stronger than this ?   And,
in truth, must one not have lost all notion of Christianity and all common sense to believe or imagine still that
Freemasonry and a belief in Christianity are com-
patible ?

[73] *Popular History of Freemasonry,* p. 517.

SECOND PART.

CAN A SERIOUS MAN, OR A MAN OF COMMON SENSE, BECOME A FREEMASON?

I ANSWER, without hesitation, *No ;* and for these reasons. I am going now to look at Freemasonry from another side, and certainly we have the right to do so ; for when a sect affects such very mighty pretensions, and proclaims itself to be neither more nor less than the illuminator and reformer of the whole human race, it is surely allowable to examine if it be really what it boasts of being ; if the high-flown praises, the emphatic admiration, and all this display of virtues which ordinarily adorn their *'pieces of architecture'* (*i.e.* Masonic speeches) are sufficiently justified ; or whether, by chance, the *'profane,'* so looked down upon it by MM. the Freemasons, would not have the right in their turn to smile instead of admiring, and to give them back both their contempt and their pity.

Nothing, in fact, can be compared with the bombast

and pomp of language which I meet with at every page of the newspapers and Masonic documents before my eyes. Freemasonry is '*divine*,' the '*lighthouse of human-ity*,' the '*sun of the world*.'

'Glory to thee, divine Freemasonry,' they exclaim. Then they sing in concert :

> '*Juste, human ain, bi n faisant, voilà ce que nous sommes ;*
> *Et le parfait Maçon est le premier des hommes.*'

(Just. humane, benevolent, that is what we are ; and a perfect Freemason is the first of men.)

The 'first of men' for virtues, for light ; this is what the Masonic banquets repeat all day long. Outside the pale of Freemasonry the human race is sunk in darkness. Freemasonry possesses all human knowledge. All wis-dom, all perfection, all virtue, all philosophy, is taught in the Masonic temples.'[1]

That is all very fine. But nevertheless when, thanks to the revelations Freemasonry has itself made, I go into its workshops and its lodges, and see the brothers at their work ; when I find men who will have neither forms of worship nor religion, nor, as they call it, 'su-

---

[1] *Le Monde-Maço nique*, t. ix. p 358.

perstitions ;' when I see all these ceremonies, all this strange and complicated hierarchy, all these signs and devices, all these marchings and countermarchings, all these singular rites ; when I hear a language unknown to the *profane;* when I assist at these initiations and mysteries, at these *works of the table* (as they call banquets), etc. etc.—I own that this 'divine' Masonry appears to me under a most astonishing aspect ;—that is the least I can say. And, in spite of my wish not to offend anybody, I cannot help thinking that all this, if it be not an antiquated veil to cover a motive which it has long been their interest to hide, is very little worthy of serious men. And Brother Félix Pyat, a revolutionist in Freemasonry as in politics, seems to me to be only reasonable when he calls these practices 'ridiculous,' 'puerile,' and 'senile.'[2]

As for me, I shall content myself with making a simple exposition of facts. I address myself to men of common sense, and common sense will judge.

[2] *Le Rappel*, quoted above.

www.ingramcontent.com/pod-product-compliance
Lightning Source LLC
Chambersburg PA
CBHW060153290526
45789CB00003B/1026